MAZE CRAZE

46 Puzzles

Albrecht Zipfel

DOVER PUBLICATIONS, INC.
New York

Bibliographical Note

Maze Craze: 46 Puzzles is a new work, first published by Dover Publications, Inc., in 1994.

International Standard Book Number: 0-486-28080-2

Manufactured in the United States of America
Dover Publications, Inc., 31 East 2nd Street, Mineola, N.Y. 11501

Life is full of riddles, and one of the most intriguing is the labyrinth.

It combines a challenge to intelligence and patience with aesthetic pleasure. This kind of experience already enthused and captivated our ancestors thousands of years ago as manifested in buildings of ancient Egypt, the palace of King Minos on Crete, Roman catacombs, medieval churches and formal English gardens. In modern games, men have always succumbed to the fascination of searching for the right path.

The labyrinth with its structure embodies at one and the same time order and chaos, intellectual knowledge and deliberate confusion.

On the way to the centre point of a labyrinth the player follows winding paths, and as he moves to and fro, back and forth, the centre point eludes him while he is already unwittingly making his way back out again. The search for a successful route thus could become a symbol of the human endeavour to reveal the hidden purpose of his existence.

A small hint to start you off! The only requisite you need for the journey through the following labyrinths and mazes is patience, a soft pencil, possibly a rubber eraser so that you can delete wrong turns and try your luck along a different route.

Do not give up too easily, since only the one who exercises his patience to the utmost will be rewarded by the sweet smell of success.

However, before you tear your hair in sheer despair: the solutions can be found beginning on page 53.

**The sphere –
a round affair**
Try to reach the centre
from one of the points A - H
around the periphery.
Although it is easier to start
from the centre, who would
cheat himself?

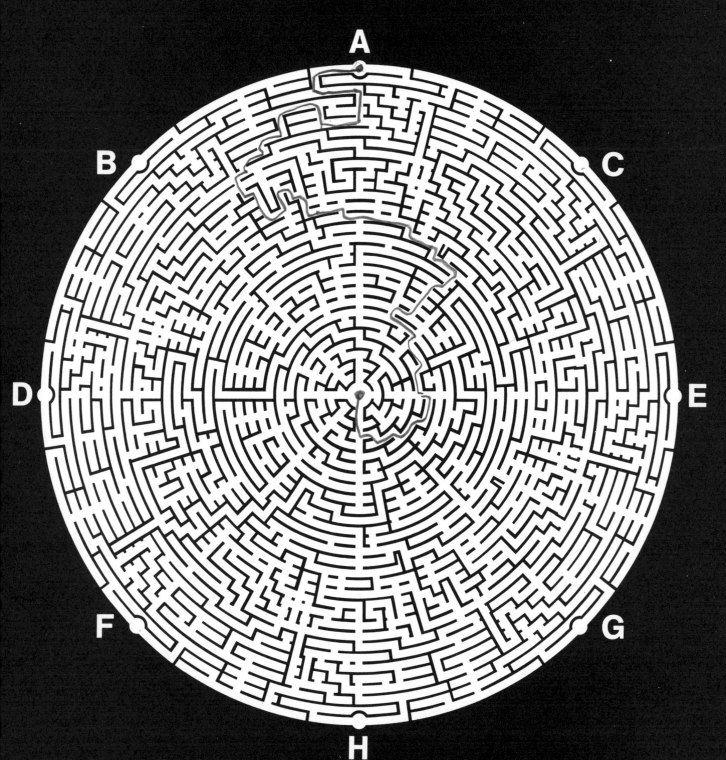

2 The triangle
with six possibilities
Which one is the correct
starting point for a successful
journey to the centre?
A, B, C, D, E or F?

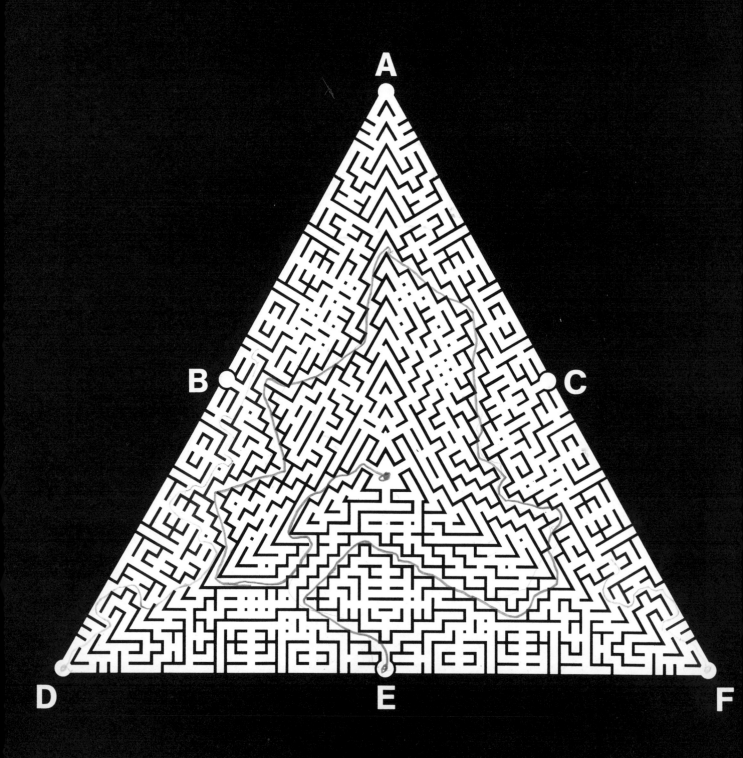

to the centre.
Only cheats will try it from
the centre outwards.

A B C

D E

F G H

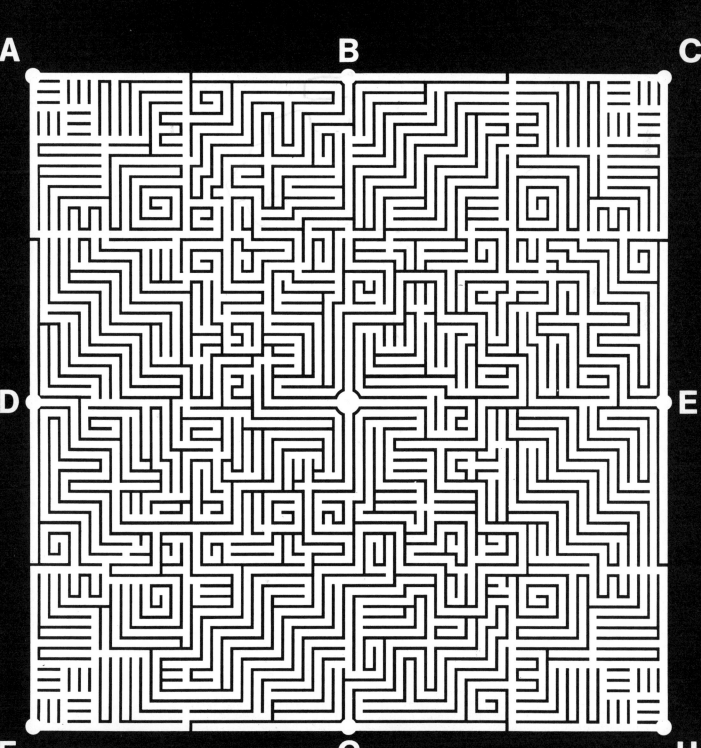

4

The hexagon – here again, the right path will lead to the goal

A,B,C,D,E,F. One of these points is the correct start on the journey to the centre. Once again, the true professional battles by fair means alone.

5 **The star –**
star among mazes
A star may lead you
along the right path from the
periphery to the centre.
If you were to try it the other
way round, you could be
disqualified.

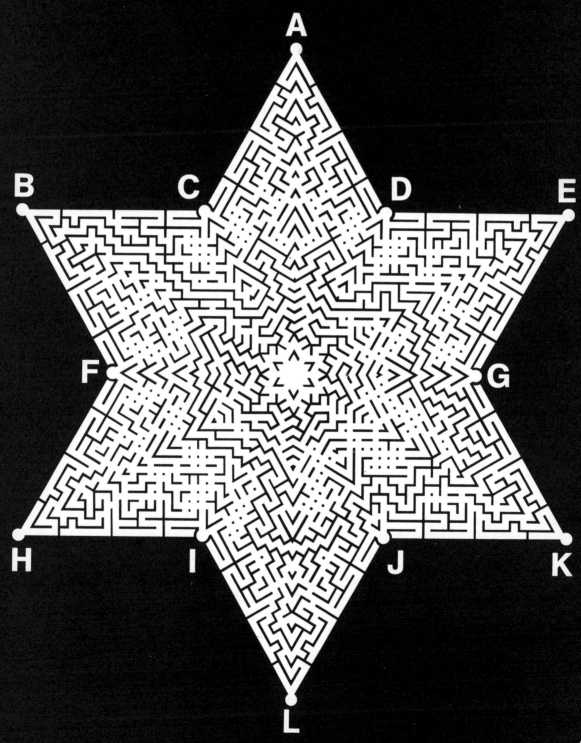

One of the six peripheral
points marks the start to a
successful route to the centre
point. It would be possible
to solve this problem the
other way around,
but, surely that would be
beneath you.

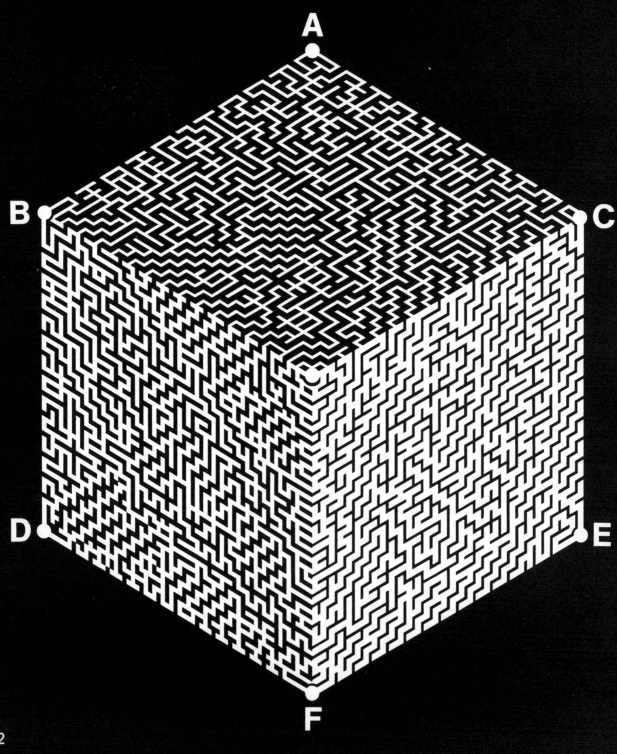

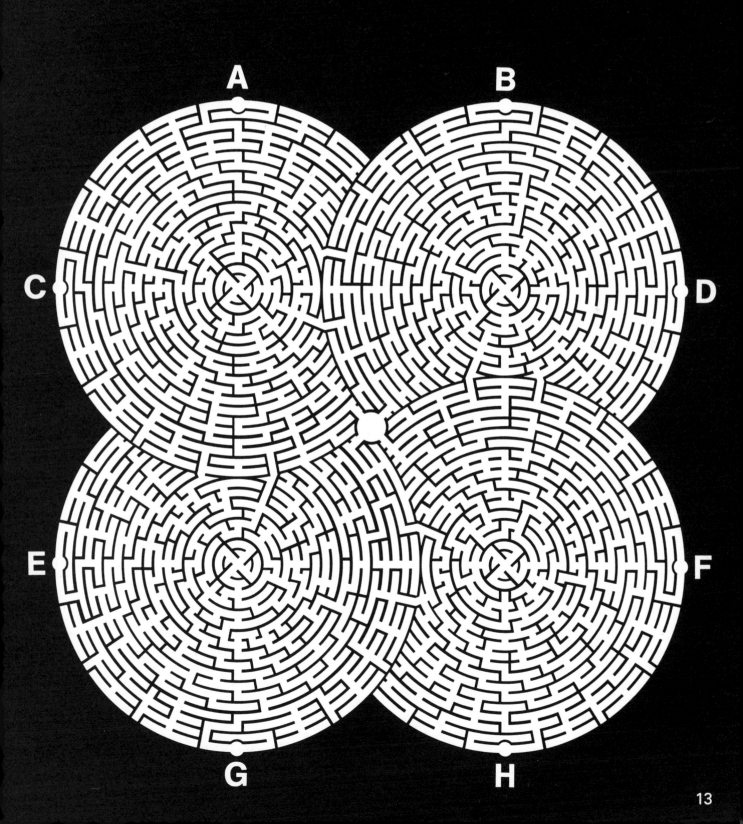

8 The clover leaf – a little luck will help here

A - H. One of these points is the correct start for the journey to the centre. It is not allowed to go from the inside outwards.

of the inner square.
Abide by the rules, never
start at the inside and try to
work your way outwards.

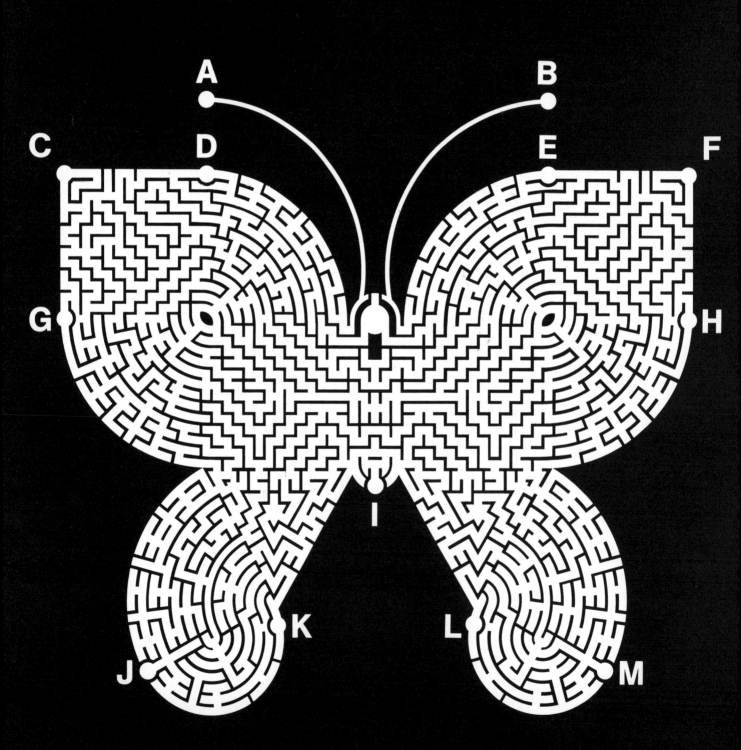

10 **The brainy butterfly**
One of the points A - M
signifies the start of
the way to the butterfly's
head. You should be
ashamed of yourself to even
try to go from the inside
outwards.

Only one of the starting points A, B, C, D, or E at the foot of the mountain leads to the summit.

A B C D E

12 The christmas tree that will enlighten you

Which one of the five routes along the tree trunk will lead you to all the candles in the right sequence (A, B, C, D, E)?

13 Snowflakes
fall from heaven
Find the correct route
from A to B but, careful, it is
very slippery. Do not stray from
the safety of the path.

14 A snowstorm - hurry to the safety of the shelter

Top, bottom, left or right, there is only one way to the shelter. We hope that you will find it before you get snowed in.

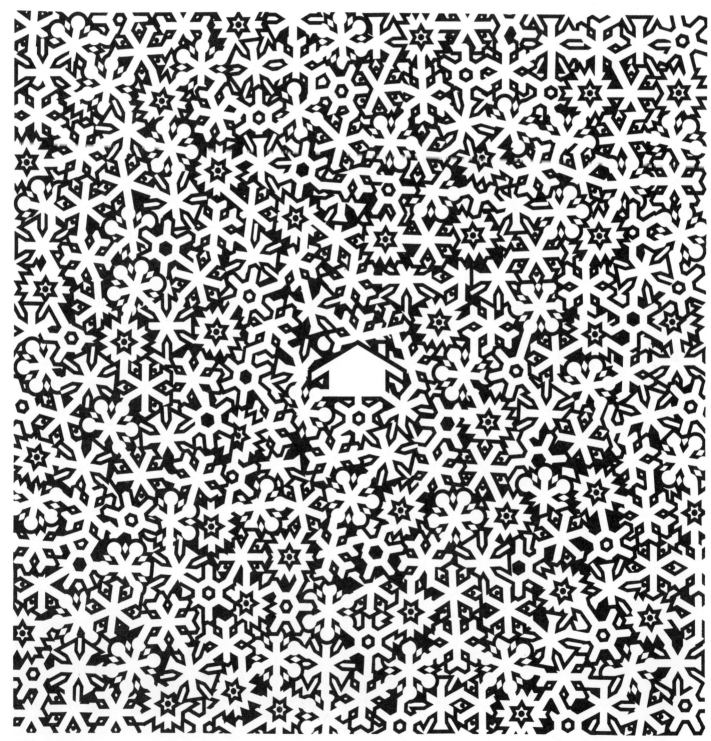

15 The numbers game - nought for nought

Look for the correct path through the jungle of numbers from 1 - 9 or the other way around.

16 Education through reading

Learn the alphabet step by step. Proceed from A to Z. It is doubtful that it will lead you to a better understanding of sophisticated literature afterwards.

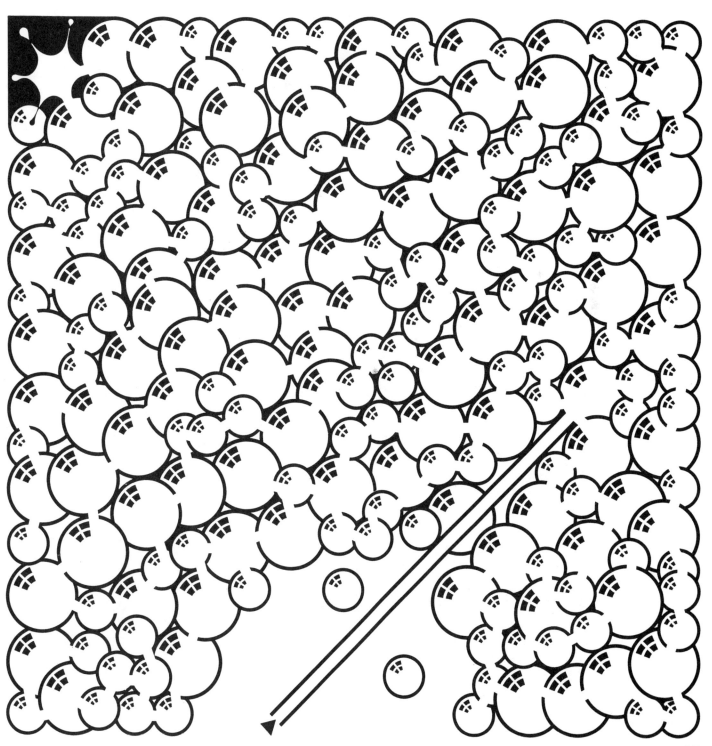

Follow the postal route of
the letter which the lover
is sending to his sweetheart.

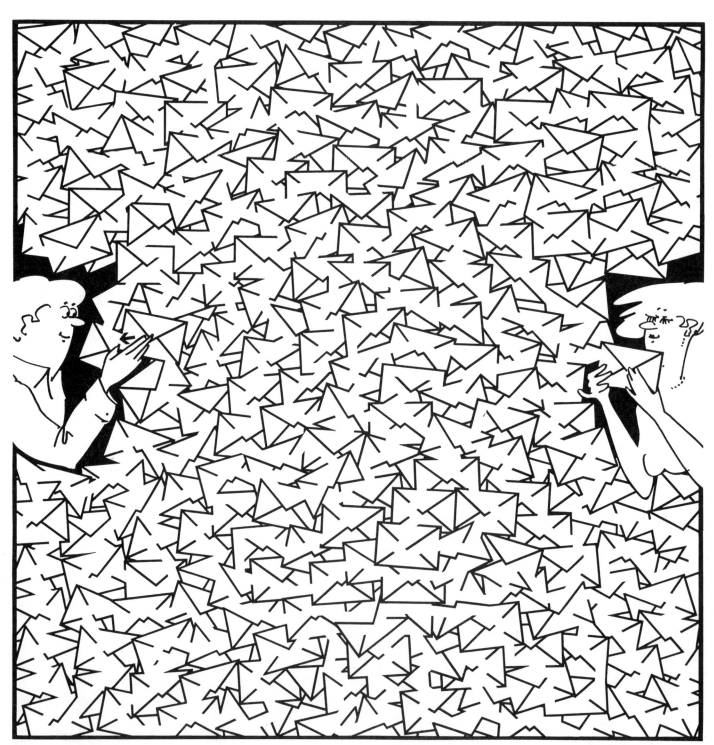

19 **From heart to heart**
Find the right way to
win the heart of your
sweetheart (from A to B).

20 Meeting in the concert hall

You are already sitting in the first row when you spot a friend in the last row (x). Try and make your way through the rows of seats to meet your friend in the interval, starting at the arrow.

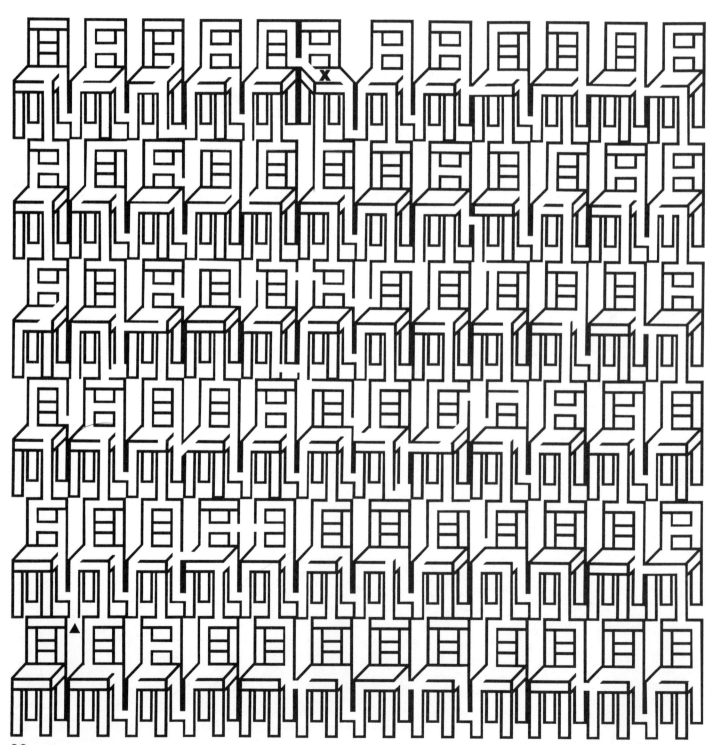

21 Dandelion seeds blowing in the wind

A gust of wind blows the seeds of the dandelion in all directions. Follow their path from the seed-vessel of the plant to the place where one seed has found the ground.

22 Meteor shower

Find the safe route starting in the top right-hand corner to the left-hand bottom corner to get through the meteor shower without injury.

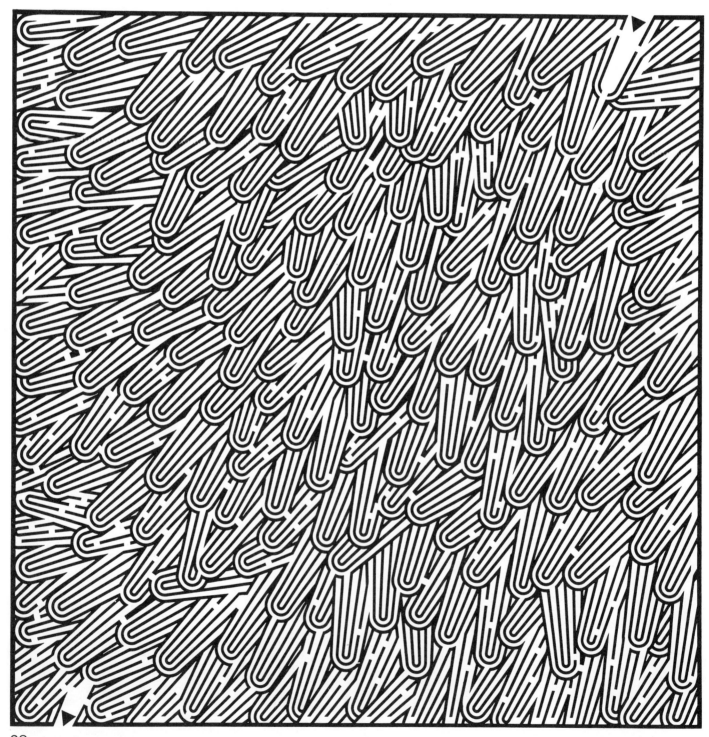

23 To the sun, sisters and brothers...

Only one way leads through an opening in one of the four sides of the cloud formation to the sun. Which one is it?

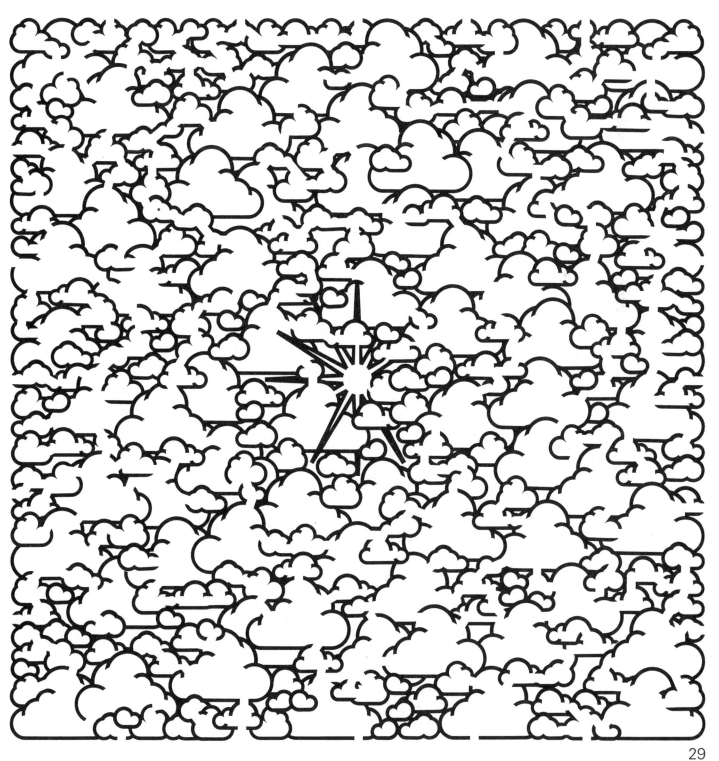

24 Safe island

Starting at the arrow try to reach the island but be careful to evade the sharks without arousing their attention.

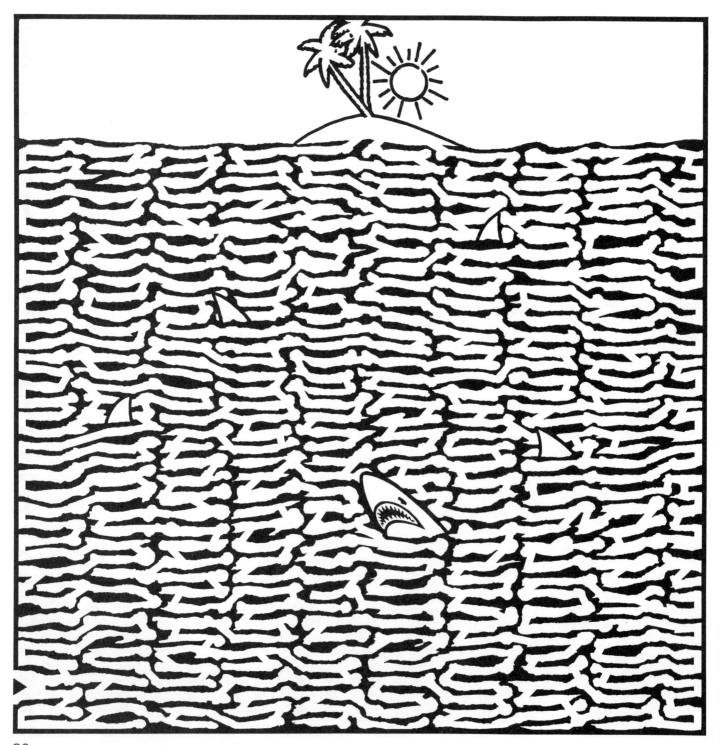

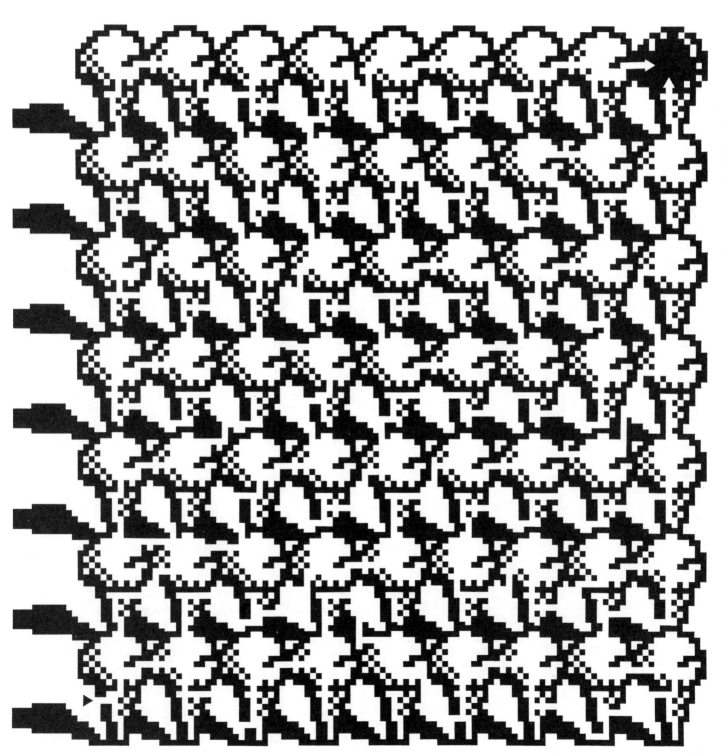

26 Into the trees, you monkeys...

One last coconut has been left in the upper left-hand corner of the palm tree. Starting at the arrow in the right-hand bottom corner, climb up the trunk and make your way across the treetops to reach the coconut.

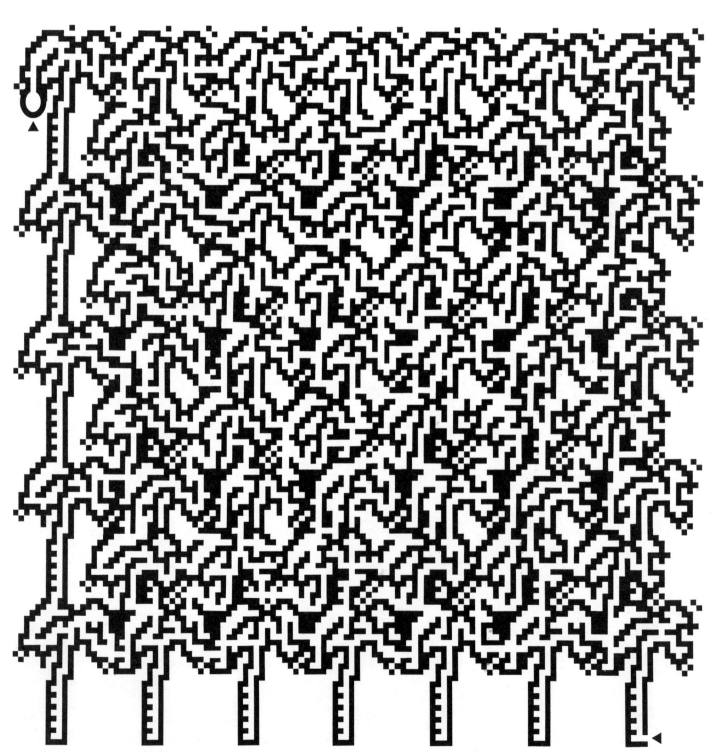

27 Pears, and yet more pears...

In order to satisfy your craving for a pineapple you will have to make your way through mountains of pears. Start from the arrow in the left-hand bottom corner.

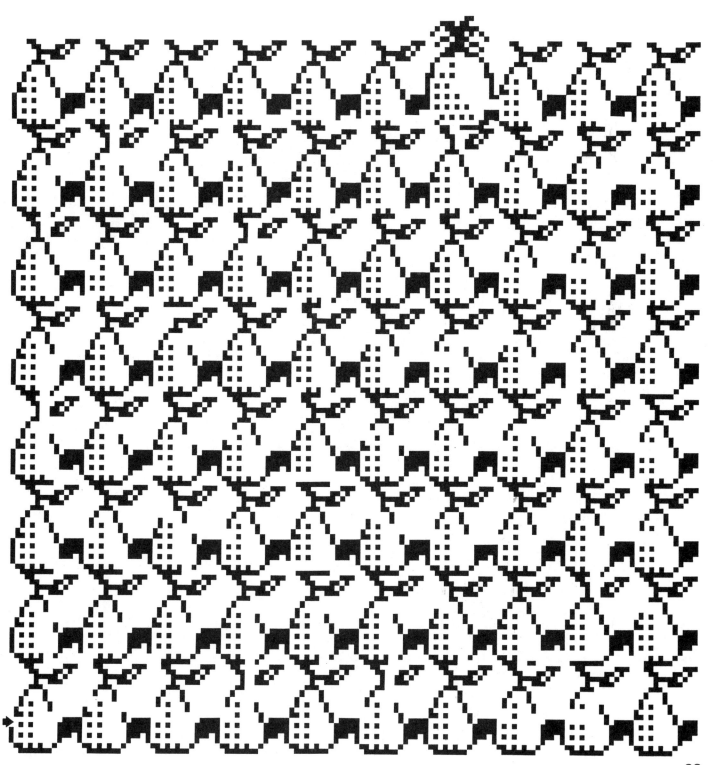

28 Terrible thirst...

After a whole night's drinking you wake up next to rows and rows of empty bottles. In order to be able to quench your thirst you will have to start at the arrow in the left-hand bottom corner to reach the only full bottle in the top row.

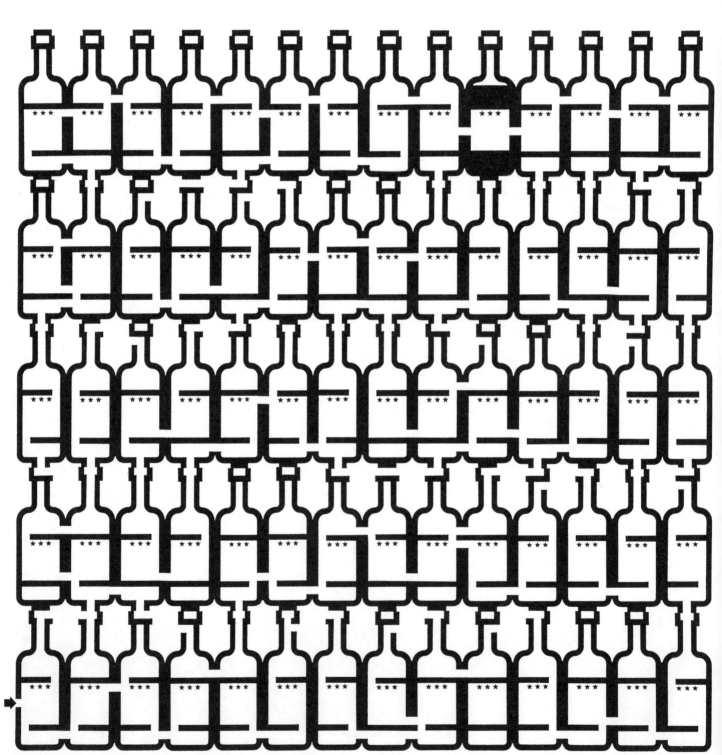

You have a date in the centre of the park, however, autumn leaves are obscuring all the paths. Find the right way, beginning at an opening in one of the four sides of the leaf-covered surface in order to get to your rendezvous in time.

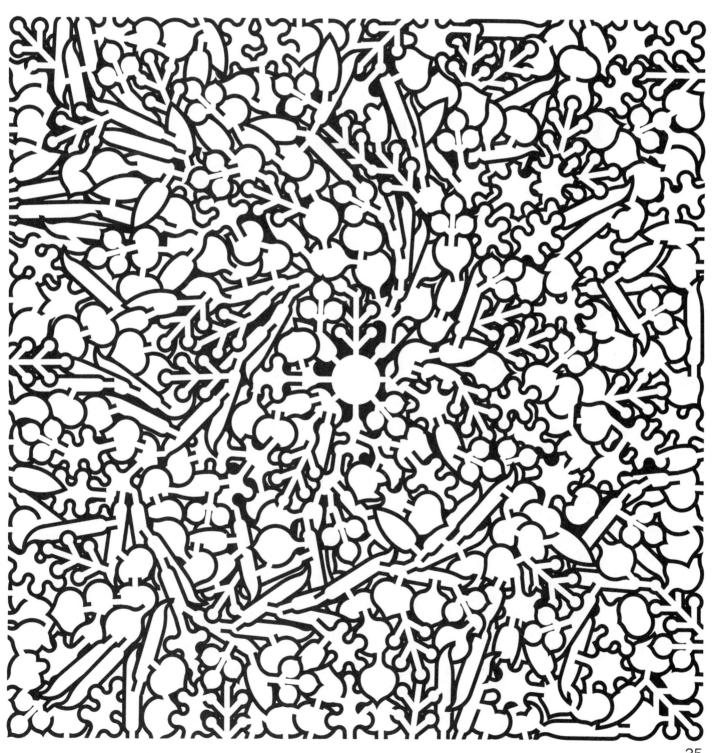

30 Barefoot in the rain

Try to find your way through the rain to reach the umbrella before you are completely soaked.
Where is the beginning? At the top, at the bottom, on the right, on the left?
There is only one way.

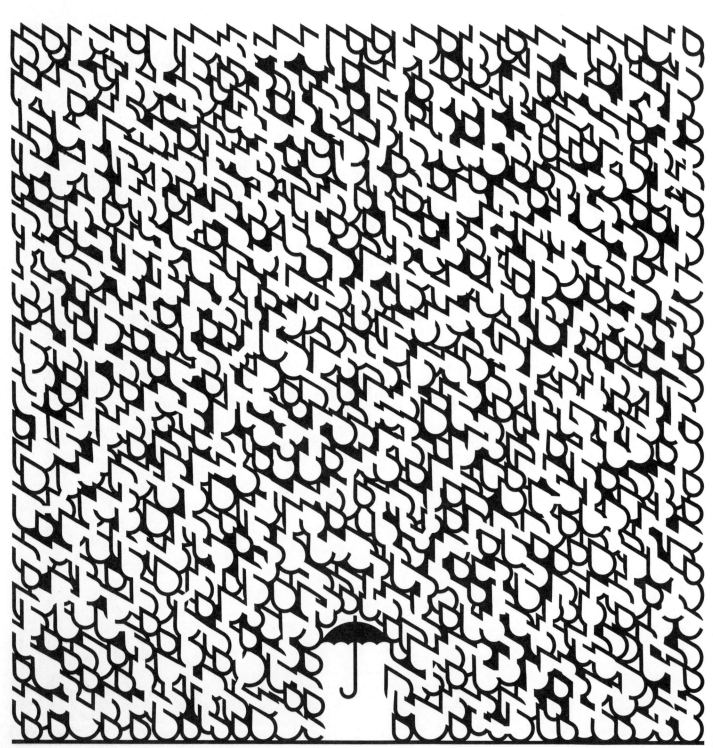

Theft at the museum
A valuable sculpture stood on a round pedestal in the centre of a square room with four doors. If you look carefully at the footprints you can ascertain through which door the thief entered the room and through which door he left it again.

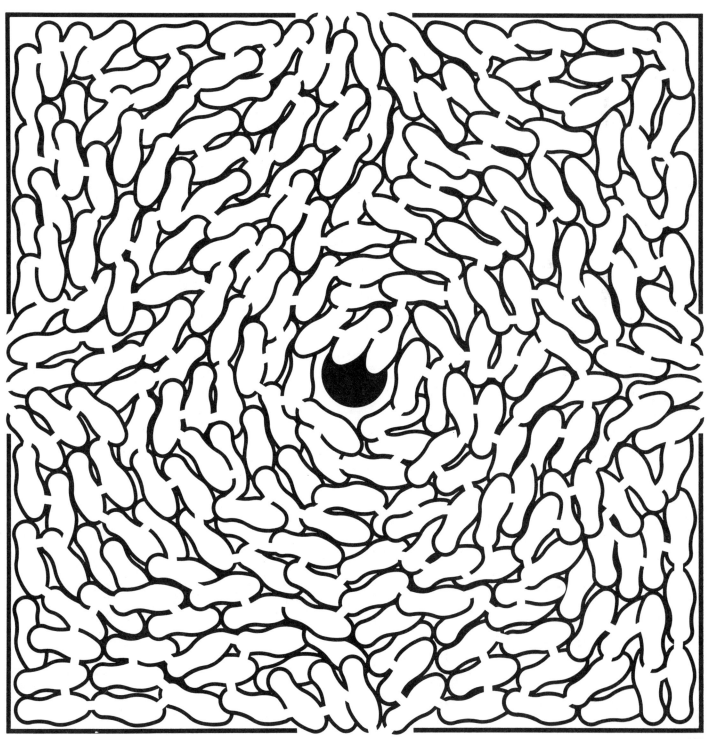

32 Battle against time

Your main task is to check that all the clocks are always set correctly. How could it have happened that the third clock from the right in row three from the top goes wrong? Hurry up and go from the arrow in the bottom left-hand corner up to correct your error.

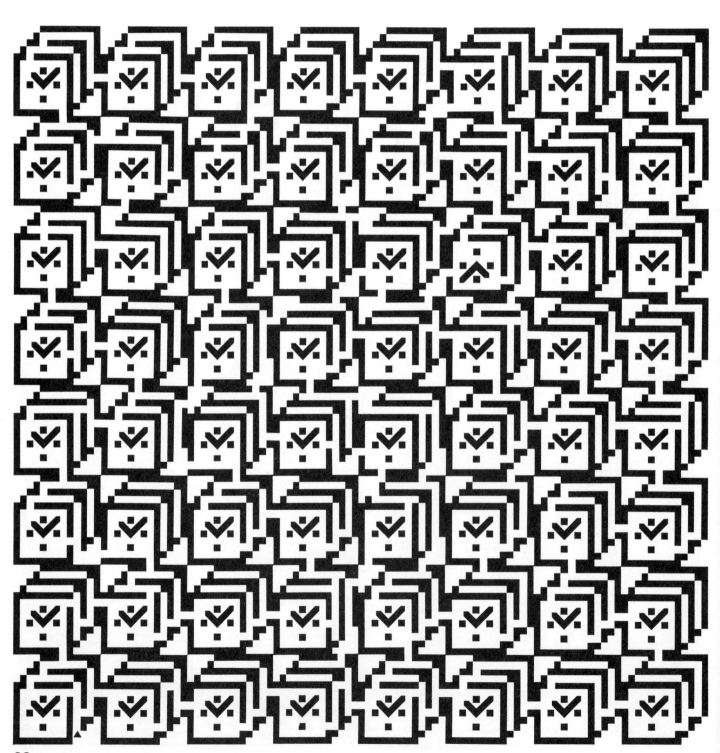

33

Turn the light on...
Disentangle the
cables in order to
ascertain which plug belongs
to which bulb.

34 The electronic age

In a conductor plate in the top left-hand corner and in the right-hand bottom corner there are three soldered spots, each connected to conductors. Find the right path to go from one corner of the circuit board diagonally via the centre to the opposite corner.

36 The path of virtue

In order to get from A to B you will have to cross innumerable courtyards where all sorts of temptations and dangers lurk. Remain steadfast and look for the shortest way to your goal.

Breakout
You are in the centre of a prison surrounded by high walls. Somebody passes you a message to the effect that a rope-ladder has been attached to one of the four walls, marked with arrows. But to which one? Take your opportunity.

38 Straight through the middle

In order to get from A to B you need to cross the centre of all five squares. It is a long journey - don't falter along the way.

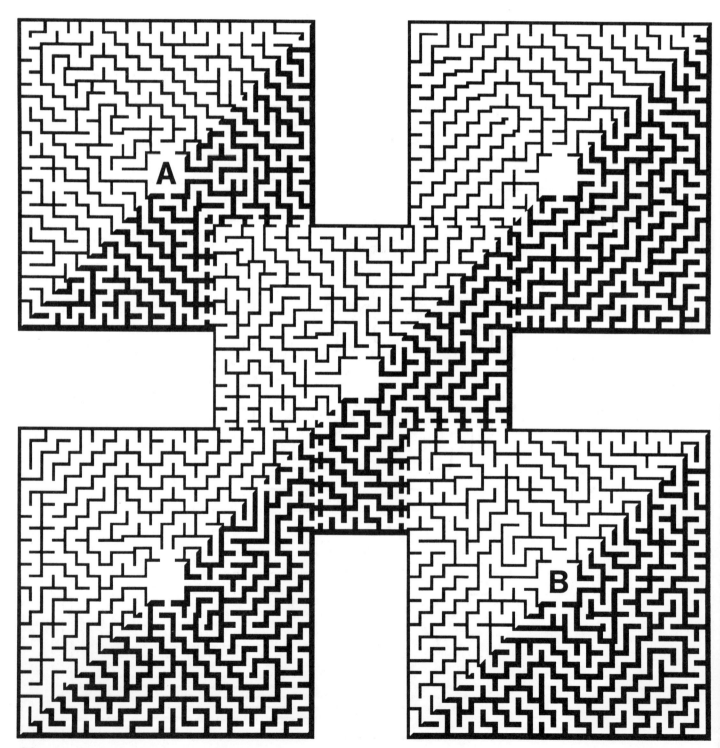

39 **Amazingly simple...**
but only if you know
the right way.
Go from A to B - not necessarily
through the centre of all
squares. It is difficult enough
as it is.

40 From left to right

Begin at the arrow on the left-hand side, overcome the cross in the centre and emerge on the right-hand side to reach the exit.

41

Variation 1
Again, the starting point is on the left-hand side. Cross the the centre circle and take care not to miss the right exit in order to leave the maze on the right-hand side again.

42 Variation 2

This time you start at the arrow on the right-hand side for a change and climb over the visible surfaces of the die in order to find, totally exhausted, the exit on the left-hand side.

**So near and
yet so far**
Try to get from A to B
or the other way around as
quickly as possible but try to
avoid dead ends.

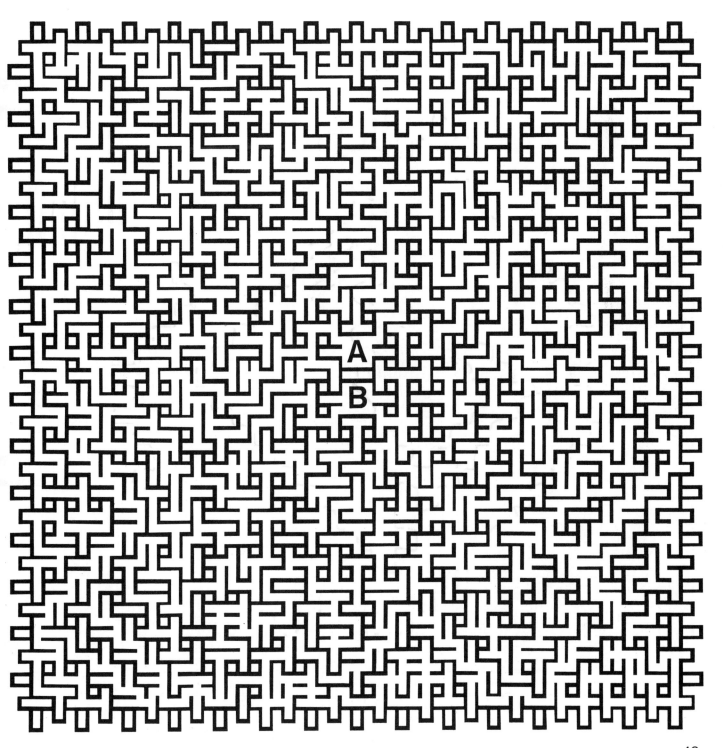

44 Round and round they go

Now to the right, now to the left you will have to go in order to get from A to B. Careful that you don't get dizzy.

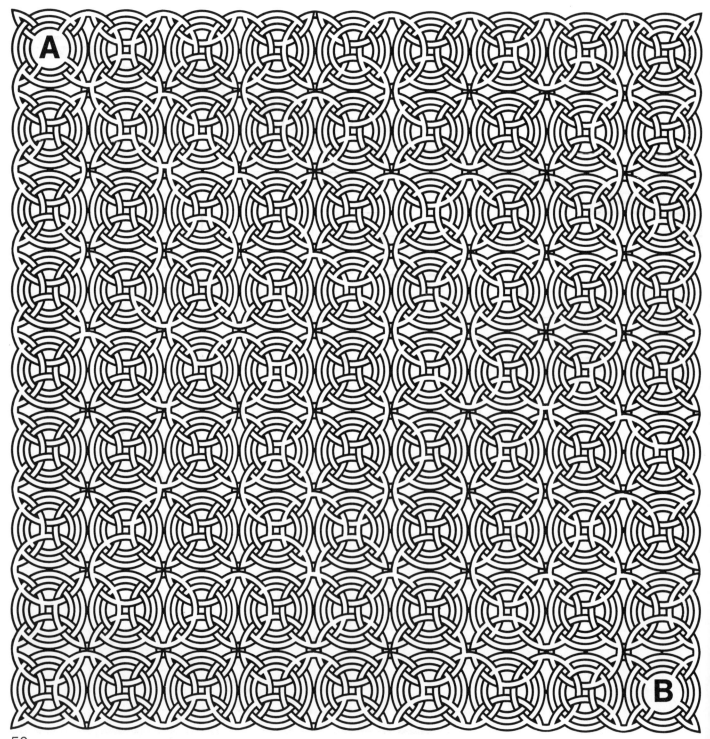

The goal in the centre is soon reached once you have found the right way, starting at one of the openings at the top, bottom, right-hand or left-hand edge.

Start from the outside to the centre or from the centre to the outside. No problem, as long as you are on the right path. In any case - all routes start at a circular opening.

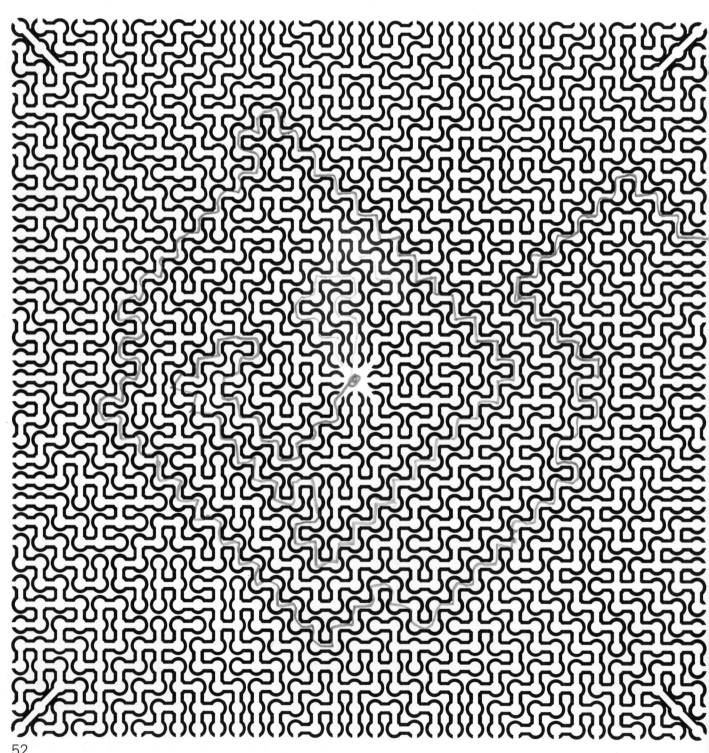

Solutions

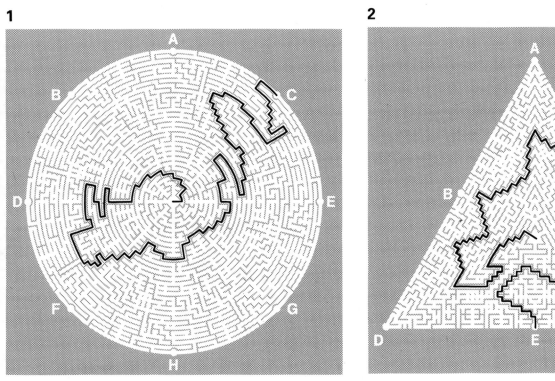

3

4

5

6

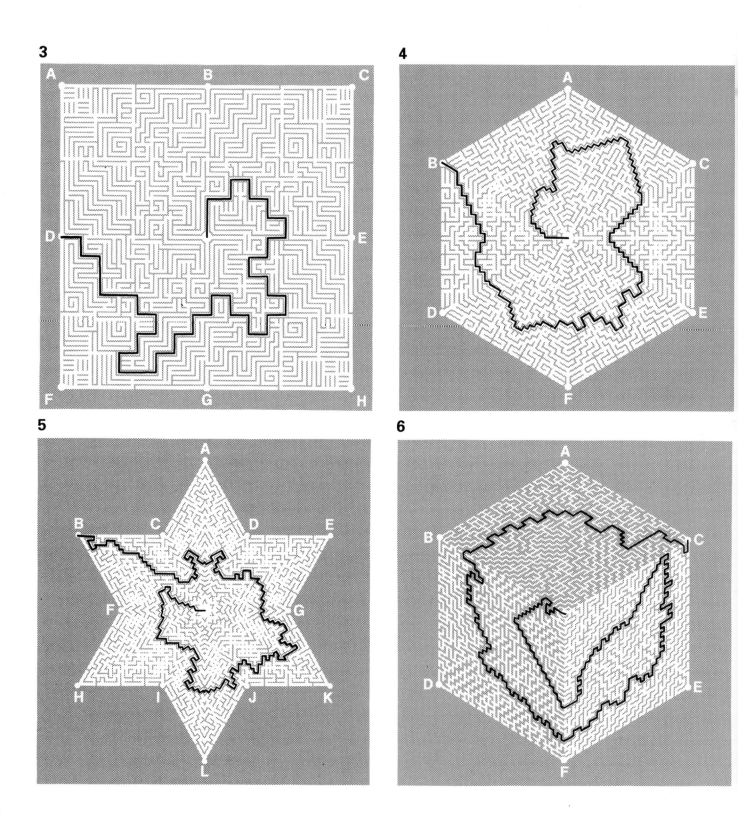

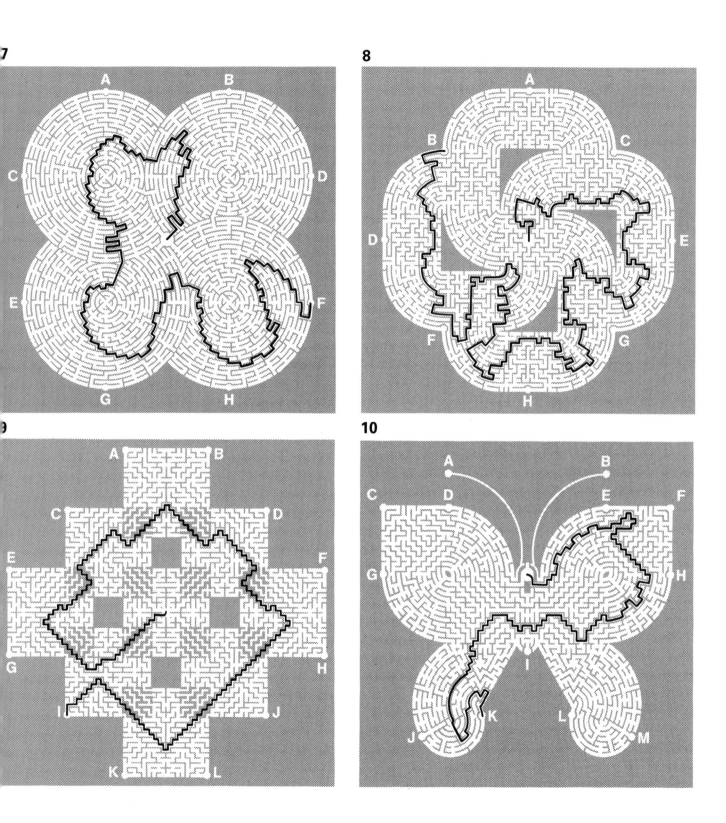

11

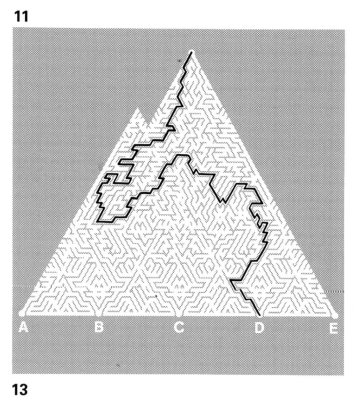

12

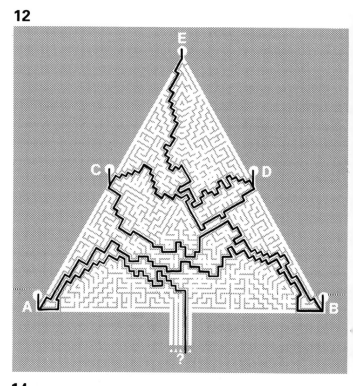

13

14

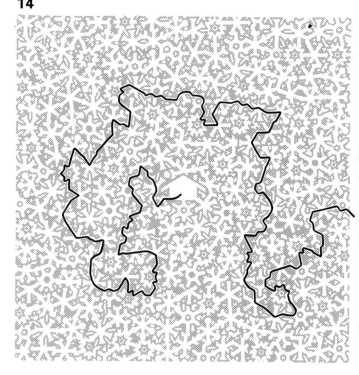

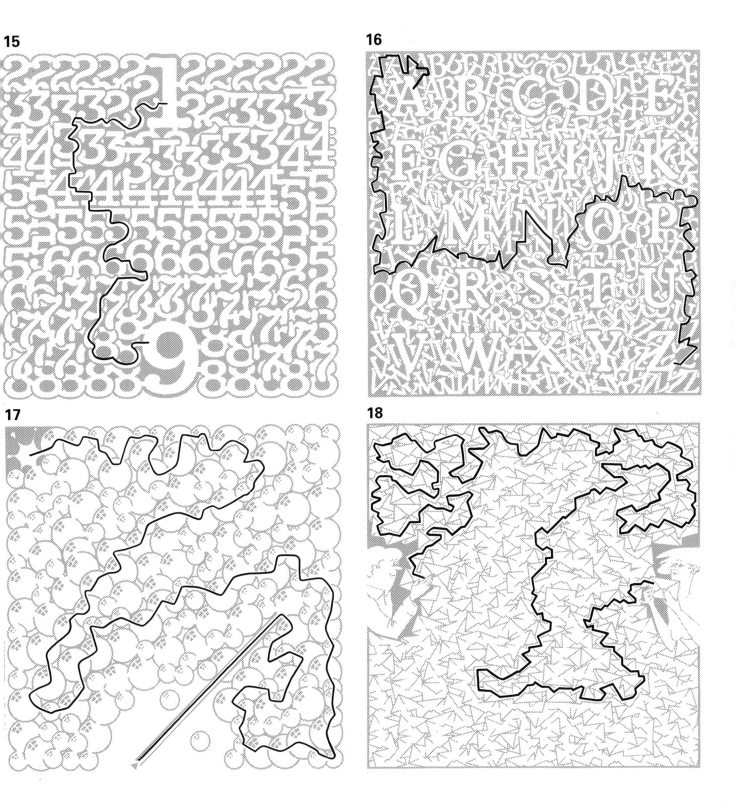

19

20

21

22

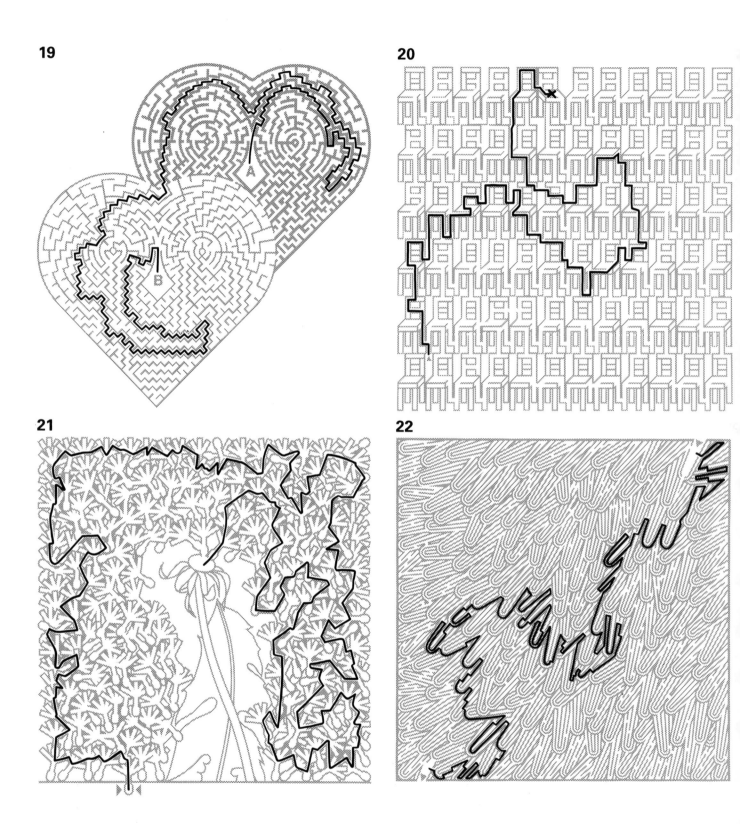

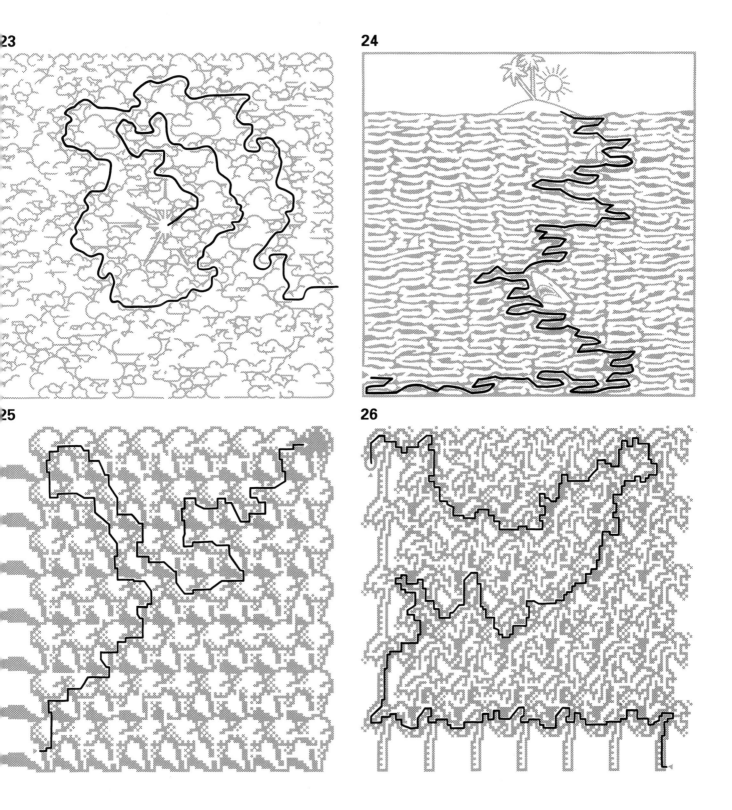

27

28

29

30

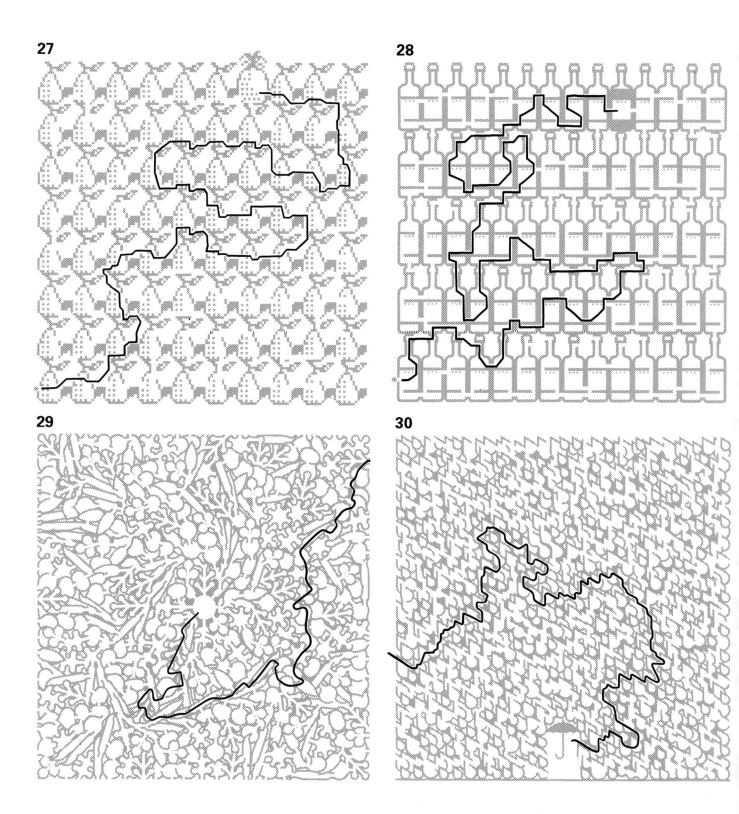

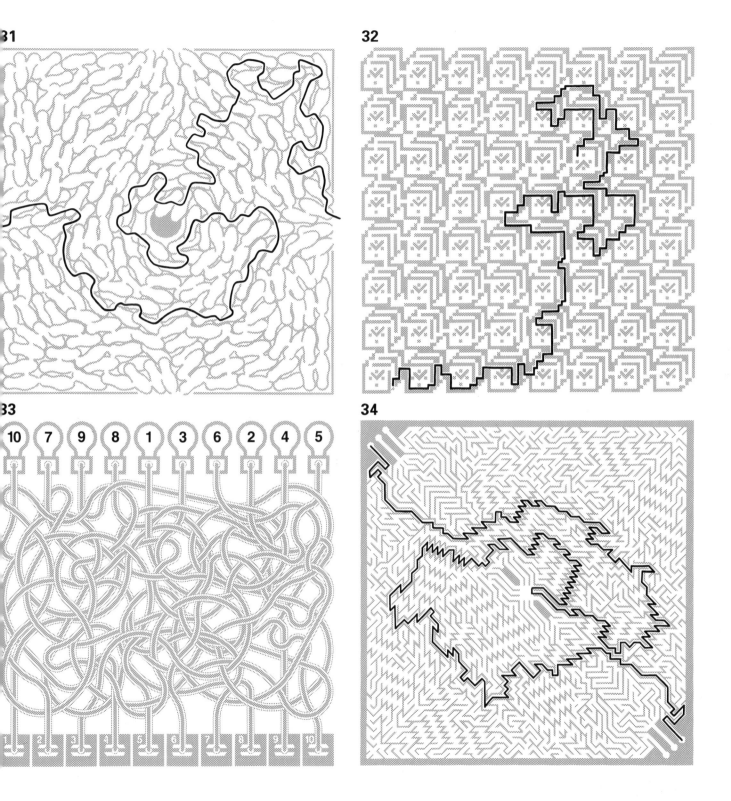

35

36

37

38

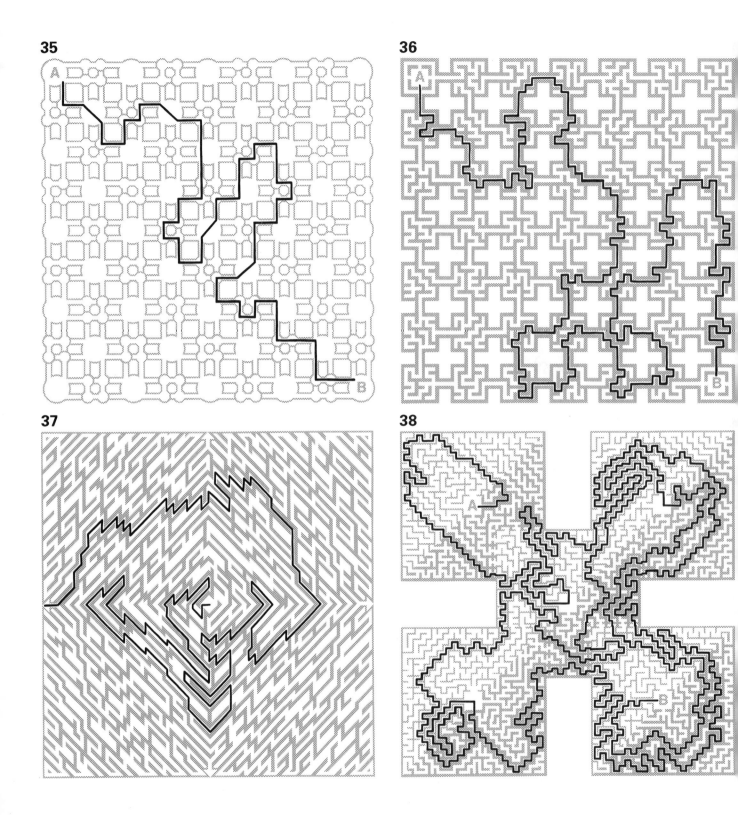

62

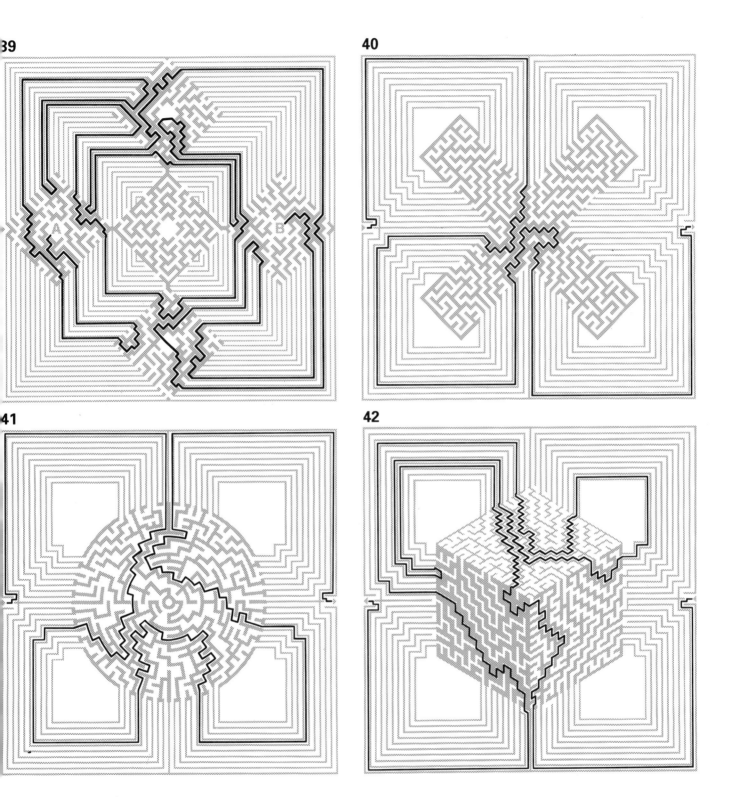

39

40

41

42

63

43

44

45

46

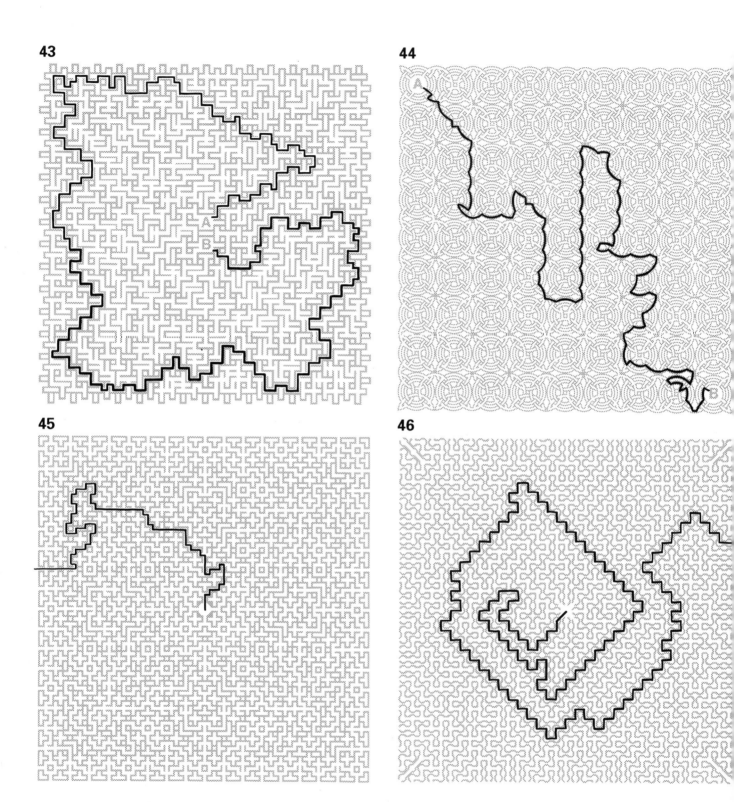